Dec 2019

BE A
CONSTRUCTION
MANAGER

GUIDE TO THE TRADES

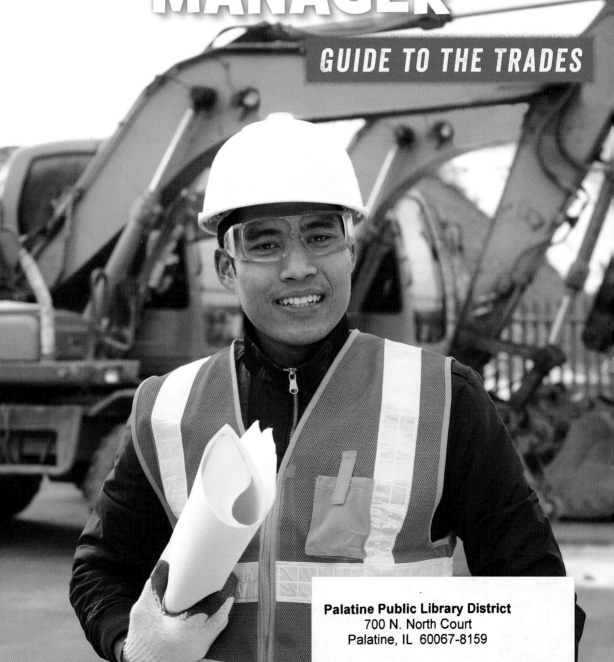

CHERRY LAKE
Publishing

Published in the United States of America by Cherry Lake Publishing
Ann Arbor, Michigan
www.cherrylakepublishing.com

Content Advisers: Laura Cotner, Professor, Joliet Junior College, Architecture, Engineering, and Construction Management;
Nancy Collins, instructor, Joliet Junior College
Reading Adviser: Marla Conn, MS, Ed., Literacy specialist, Read-Ability, Inc.

Photo Credits: Cover and page 1, ©ndoeljindoel/Shutterstock; page 5, ©Diego Cervo/Shutterstock; page 6, ©sirtravelot/
Shutterstock; page 8, ©PRPicturesProduction/Shutterstock; page 10, ©bernatets photos/Shutterstock; page 13, ©Gorodenkoff/
Shutterstock; page 14, ©Chia_kaow_photo/Shutterstock; page 16, ©ESB Professional/Shutterstock; page 19, ©YP_Studio/
Shutterstock; page 20, ©SrdjanVrebac/Shutterstock; page 22, ©Cineberg/Shutterstock; page 25, ©Jat306/Shutterstock;
page 26, ©CHAIYA/Shutterstock; page 28, ©thansak253700/Shutterstock

Library of Congress Cataloging-in-Publication Data
Names: Mara, Wil, author.
Title: Be a construction manager / by Wil Mara.
Description: Ann Arbor, Michigan : Cherry Lake Publishing, [2019] | Series:
  21st century skills library | Includes bibliographical references and
  index.
Identifiers: LCCN 2019003504| ISBN 9781534148246 (lib. bdg.) | ISBN
  9781534149670 (pdf) | ISBN 9781534151109 (pbk.) | ISBN 9781534152533
  (ebook)
Subjects: LCSH: Building—Vocational guidance.
Classification: LCC TH159 .M373 2019 | DDC 690.023—dc23
LC record available at https://lccn.loc.gov/2019003504

Cherry Lake Publishing would like to acknowledge the work of The Partnership for 21st Century Learning.
Please visit *www.p21.org* for more information.

Printed in the United States of America
Corporate Graphics

ABOUT THE AUTHOR

Wil Mara is the author of over 175 fiction and nonfiction books for children. He has written
many titles for Cherry Lake Publishing, including the popular *Global Citizens: Modern Media*
and *Citizen's Guide* series. More about his work can be found at www.wilmara.com.

TABLE OF CONTENTS

CHAPTER 1

A Busy Day

Bill Cress wakes up well before sunrise. After a short shower and even shorter breakfast, he's out the door and on the road. The day's job **site**, where a new office complex is being built, is less than 15 minutes away. Bill's phone starts ringing before he even gets there. The woman at the other end of the call is one of the people paying for the new building. She and her partners are investing millions of dollars in this project, so they want everything to go smoothly. And Bill is in charge of making sure that happens. He's a construction manager, which means he oversees building projects from beginning to end.

A construction manager often spends a lot of time in meetings or on phone calls.

Bill can hear in the investor's voice that she is a little upset. He knew this call was coming because one of the pipes in the new building's plumbing system developed a leak overnight. The investor doesn't understand how brand-new pipes could leak. She begins to calm down as Bill explains that it's because they're doing this project during the winter months. Cold weather can cause all sorts of problems with new construction, including leaky seals in plumbing connections. But because

Construction managers deal directly with many different types of workers to complete each project.

the investors wanted the building finished by a certain date, Bill's crew had no choice but to work through the winter. Bill assures the investor that the leak is an easy problem to fix. It will take very little time and will not slow down the overall progress of the project. He promises to send her a text and some photos of the repaired pipe as soon as it is fixed.

The moment Bill gets to the job site, there are already several teams waiting to talk to him. Each is in charge of a different part of the project. He speaks to the plumbing team first and is happy to learn that their manager has already put together a plan to fix the leaky pipe. Bill sends them off to take care of it and turns his attention to the other teams.

The carpentry workers are concerned because a delivery of floorboards is two days late. Bill puts them to work on one of the building's two elevator shafts while they wait for the

21st Century Content

There are about 400,000 construction managers working in the United States. The states that employ the most are listed here:

- California: 32,780
- Texas: 25,630
- Florida: 22,130
- New York: 12,150
- Illinois: 10,140

Even though construction managers move from one job site to another as they complete projects, they also have offices where they can take care of business tasks.

boards to arrive. The masonry team finished the basement walls a day early and wants to know what to do now. Bill tells them to start working on the front walkway. The electrical team is worried that the wiring they need to power each office will end up costing more than they originally estimated. Bill determines exactly how much higher the cost will be and decides that it will still fit within the project's budget.

Bill's office is inside a small trailer on the job site. Once he finally gets inside, he pours a cup of coffee. Then he sits at his desk and looks over the building's **blueprints**. He thinks back to when they were first drawn. He had worked with the architects to make a variety of changes. These changes had ended up saving a lot of money for the building's investors. Bill has been managing new construction projects for over 20 years, and he's very well paid for reasons just like this. In fact, he's been making more than $100,000 per year for a while now. It's not unusual for a construction manager to earn this much. The average pay for his profession is around $91,000 per year, and the annual job growth is about 11 percent, which is higher than most other industries. This means there is always plenty of work to go around for skilled managers.

After Bill finishes looking at the blueprints, he picks up his notepad. It contains a to-do list he made the day before. He has to review a few **contracts**, order some building materials, sign a pile of paychecks, and perform a safety check of the entire site. He also has to meet with some people on the town council about building **codes**. Bill keeps adding to his to-do list as the day goes on. There are times when it feels like he'll never get to the end of it. But this is all part of the challenge of

Every day is filled with new challenges for a construction manager.

being a construction manager, and Bill loves it. The job is never boring because there's always plenty to do, and every day presents new challenges to be resolved. Bill is a natural problem solver and leader. The people who work for him trust and respect him. So do the people who've hired him. And when these office buildings are finally finished, Bill knows they'll be done right.

CHAPTER 2

Becoming a Construction Manager

The path to becoming a construction manager is somewhat different from that of other careers in the construction industry. Most of the people involved in the hands-on aspects of construction work in the trades. They perform the actual work involved in building new structures, such as carpentry, masonry, plumbing, electrical wiring, and paving. Construction managers, on the other hand, are involved more in supervising the overall construction process.

Working as a construction manager requires a very different set of skills from doing hands-on labor. For example, a construction manager might only know a little bit about carpentry. But it is the manager's job to make sure the carpenters

A college degree is usually an important first step toward a career as a construction manager.

have all the materials and equipment they need, know their assignments every day, and are working in safe conditions.

Most construction managers these days need a college degree to be considered for steady employment. Putting up a new home or building is more complex than ever, and many schools now offer degrees in construction management. There are more than 50 schools in the United States with two-year associate's degree programs, and more than 100 offer four-year bachelor's degrees. A few even offer master's degrees.

Business, math, and writing skills are all essential for a good manager.

Construction management students take courses in construction methods, engineering, and construction-related sciences. They learn about different building materials and how to estimate the costs of different projects. They also learn local building codes and study design and architecture.

In addition to construction-related topics, students learn general business and management skills. For example, they will find out how to write and read contracts, build good relationships with employees, and resolve conflicts. Perhaps

14

most importantly, they will learn the basic principles of **project management**.

Construction management students also study general mathematics and statistics. Math is a big part of life on the job. It helps construction managers take measurements, estimate costs, and manage budgets. Mathematical mistakes in construction can be very costly, so managers need to be confident of their skills.

Beyond formal classroom education, aspiring construction managers also need some on-the-job work experience. This can be gained in a number of ways. Some construction managers begin their careers working in the trades. They may work at a particular trade for many years while gaining some management experience as they go. Or they might try a variety of trades in order to broaden their skill set. The best managers know how to manage people and juggle many different details, and they have some understanding of each of the trades involved in construction. General knowledge of the trades will help managers keep a firm grasp on their projects and enable them to communicate clearly with the workers they oversee.

An experienced mentor can be a valuable source of knowledge for managers who are just beginning their careers.

Many companies are willing to provide on-the-job training to new hires with construction management degrees. Qualified applicants will not immediately become head project managers, of course. Instead, they will typically take part in an **apprenticeship** program. During this period, the budding manager is **mentored** by a construction manager with many years of experience and may be given the title of junior or assistant manager. This apprenticeship can last anywhere from several months to two or three years, depending on the company and position the candidate is seeking.

Life and Career Skills

Though it is not required by law, some construction managers choose to become certified. Certification is awarded by professional associations such as the Construction Management Association of America and the American Institute of Constructors. To become certified, managers typically need a certain amount of on-site job experience. They also need to pass a test proving their knowledge of the profession.

Becoming a certified construction manager can lead to future job opportunities. It offers proof to potential employers that a manager is both experienced and knowledgeable.

CHAPTER 3

On the Job

About 38 percent of all construction managers are self-employed. This means they own their own businesses. Someone who wants to construct a building might hire one of these freelance managers to oversee the project. Some managers work mainly on home construction projects. Others work on nonresidential buildings, such as offices, schools, and hospitals.

It takes a certain type of personality combined with a certain set of skills to be an effective construction manager. For example, people who tend to be highly organized will often do well as managers. Even a minor construction project involves literally hundreds of details, and the manager has to stay on top of all of them. What makes this even more challenging is that

Construction managers must be able to juggle several tasks at once and solve problems as they arise.

these details are all connected. One unexpected problem can trigger a dozen others. For example, the manager has to be sure all the materials for the project are delivered on time. If one delivery isn't made, then work may have to be halted for the day. Delaying one aspect of the project could delay others in turn. The entire schedule could be thrown off. A well-organized manager can avoid such problems by keeping careful track of details. Good managers also have backup plans in place in case something goes wrong.

Construction managers must be able to read blueprints and other technical documents to do their jobs effectively.

Managers play a key role in planning a new construction project. For example, a manager will help determine a project's budget. Experienced construction managers will be able to guide owners toward a realistic cost estimate. They can explain the different parts of the total cost, including labor, materials, and permits. The manager will also determine the areas where costs can and cannot be trimmed.

To plan effectively, managers use their knowledge of general architecture and construction principles. For example, an experienced manager will know which materials are best for each aspect of the job and where they can be acquired. A manager may also be the one who writes up the detailed proposal that is submitted for final approval before actual construction begins.

Good construction managers need excellent leadership skills, too. They will be overseeing not only the project itself

21st Century Content

There are several different types of construction managers. Each has the same general responsibilities, but they work in different environments and on different types of projects. As a result, some construction management jobs pay a little better than others. According to the U.S. Bureau of Labor Statistics, these are the most common categories of construction management and the average salaries they bring:

- Heavy and civil engineering construction: $95,630
- Nonresidential building construction: $93,080
- Specialty trade contracting: $86,830
- Residential building construction: $84,620

A good manager should be skilled at explaining complicated situations in a clear and precise way.

but also a large group of workers. These workers include tradesmen, suppliers, and lower-level managers. Construction managers also have to be able to work professionally with the building team. They must keep the people who are paying for a building informed of the job's ongoing progress. This sometimes means explaining delays and cost overruns. To this end, personal skills are very important. A manager must be a good listener as well as an effective communicator.

Communication abilities are particularly important because workers have to know exactly what needs to be done each day. Similarly, a construction manager should be able to resolve conflicts between two or more parties. Construction work can be unpredictable and stressful at times. It is the manager's job to make sure employees work as a team. This also means knowing how to sense when workers are in need of praise or break time.

Another trait that all construction managers should possess is the ability to resolve problems as quickly as possible. Because problems can occur at the most unpredictable moments, the manager is usually on call at all times. In fact, about one in every three managers can expect to work more than 40 hours per week.

When a problem arises, a manager must first analyze the situation to locate the cause. The next step is figuring out a solution so work can continue. For example, if a crane stops working and a mechanic is not available to fix it, the manager might call another company to supply a working crane as soon as possible.

CHAPTER 4

Rules and Regulations

There are many legal issues involved in construction. In fact, these issues have become so complex that there is an entire specialty in the legal profession known as construction law. Construction managers will need to be familiar with the laws and legal contracts that govern their profession. There's a good chance they'll have to deal with these legal issues directly at some point.

Construction managers need to be very familiar with local building codes. Building codes are rules, laws, and other guidelines that determine exactly how a building can and cannot be constructed. Codes are put in place for many reasons. They make sure buildings are safe for people to use.

When managers spot a potential code violation or some other issue, they must work quickly to solve the problem.

They also ensure that buildings are environmentally friendly and do not cause problems for neighboring structures.

Ignoring building codes can put people at risk. For example, asbestos is a material that was once widely used in new construction. Over time, however, it was discovered to cause a variety of serious health problems. Today, the use of asbestos is almost always a violation of building codes. Similarly, many paints used to contain lead, which proved to

It takes a great deal of money, resources, and labor to construct a new building.

be dangerous to human health. Today, lead paints are rarely used in any type of construction due to code regulations. It is part of a construction manager's responsibilities to make sure that all work being done on a job site meets the most current building codes, as shown on the blueprints.

A construction manager also has to stay on top of all issues relating to insurance. This means they must seek out insurance policies, understand their terms, and pay the **premiums** on time. Insurance is important to have on any construction project. If something goes wrong on the job that results in significant damage, insurance helps cover the cost of those losses.

Negotiating contracts is another everyday part of the construction manager's job. There are at least two sides to

Life and Career Skills

Construction can be a dangerous industry. Tools, materials, and other equipment can all pose safety hazards. Workers could fall from heights or be burned or electrocuted. Thankfully, most of these dangers can be easily avoided by following safety standards. Construction managers are responsible for ensuring that a job site is as safe as possible. They must perform inspections to make sure workers are wearing the appropriate safety gear, taking the proper precautions, and more.

Making deals and building relationships with colleagues is a big part of a construction manager's job.

every negotiation, and each will want to secure the best terms. Skilled managers work to satisfy all the parties involved as much as possible. This is a talent that develops after many years of experience.

A manager also needs to be prepared for the occasional legal dispute over contracts. Subcontracting is the practice of hiring different groups to do different jobs. There might be, for example, one contract for the carpenters, one for the plumbers, one for the electricians, and so on. Sometimes workers do not meet the terms of a contract. For example, workers might perform their job incorrectly, costing owners money to fix the problems. Or they might fail to meet deadlines. In these cases, the construction manager may have to take legal action.

Think About It

Humans have been building things for thousands of years. As far back as the Neolithic period, which began around 10,000 BCE, people were erecting simple structures in order to shelter themselves.

Among history's most famous construction projects were the pyramids of ancient Egypt. Masons chiseled huge stone blocks, then workers dragged the blocks to the building sites. After that, the pyramids were assembled one block at a time. Most of them took decades to build. What do you think it was like to oversee the construction of one of these amazing structures? What problems were likely the most common? How do you suppose those problems were best solved?

Now think about what it would be like to be a construction manager today. Which parts of the job would you enjoy the most? Which parts would you enjoy the least? Explain your answers.

Find Out More

BOOKS

Duke, Shirley. *Pyramids of Egypt*. Vero Beach, FL: Rourke Educational Media, 2015.

Koontz, Robin. *Think Like an Engineer*. Vero Beach, FL: Rourke Educational Media, 2017.

Rhatigan, Joe. *Get a Job at a Construction Site*. Ann Arbor, MI: Cherry Lake Publishing, 2017.

WEBSITES

PBS—Building Big
www.pbs.org/wgbh/buildingbig
Learn more about what it takes to construct large structures such as bridges, dams, and skyscrapers.

U.S. Bureau of Labor Statistics—Occupational Outlook Handbook: Construction Managers
https://www.bls.gov/ooh/management/construction-managers.htm
Learn how to become a construction manager and more about the profession at this government site.

GLOSSARY

apprenticeship (uh-PREN-tis-ship) a training situation in which someone learns a skill by working with an expert on the job

blueprints (BLOO-printz) drawings that illustrate how a structure needs to be built

codes (KOHDZ) rules that determine the correct design and construction of buildings

contracts (KAHN-trakts) written business agreements between two or more parties

mentored (MEN-tord) taught by a more experienced person

premiums (PREE-mee-uhmz) the amounts of money that must be paid to secure an insurance policy

project management (PRAH-jekt MAN-ij-muhnt) the process of overseeing a project to ensure that it runs smoothly and reaches the desired end result

site (SITE) location of a construction project

INDEX